WHAT ABOUT DIVORCE?

The One Guide To Read Before Filing For Divorce In Arizona.

Ariano & Reppucci, PLLC

ARIANO & REPPUCCI

Ryan M. Reppucci, Esquire
Ariano & Reppucci, PLLC
1430 East Missouri Avenue
Suite B-127
Phoenix, Arizona 85014
(844) Read-Law
readlaw@attorneys-arizona.com

CONTENTS

THE AUTHOR

The path leading to Ryan M. Reppucci's current status as one of Phoenix's leading family law attorneys is filled with numerous honors and awards. After graduating from Arizona State with highest honors and inclusion in one of America's most prestigious student honor societies, he attended University of Detroit Mercy School of Law where his decorated career included receiving the *University of Detroit Mercy School of Law Book Award,* nomination for membership in *Who's Who Among Students in American Colleges and Universities,* and membership in the *University of Detroit Mercy School of Law Moot Court*. He was awarded the degree of *Juris Doctor* in 2008.

He began his law career with the fabled Wayne County Prosecutor's Office where he obtained valuable experience serving in a wide variety of roles in one of this country's busiest criminal court systems.

His success with the prosecutor's office resulted in his being offered a clerkship with the Law Office of Cripps & Silver, one of Detroit's leading criminal defense firms. After a year in this position, Mr. Reppucci chose to return to Phoenix and fulfill his professional dream of creating one of Phoenix's most respected family law firms.

Mr. Reppucci—a member of the State Bar of Arizona, the State Bar of Arizona's Family Law Section, and the United States District Court for the District of Arizona—has experienced great success during his family law career in Phoenix that began in 2009. The law office of *Ariano & Reppucci* he co-founded with Christopher H. Ariano has helped thousands of clients achieve excellent outcomes and has been so successful that it now boasts several locations throughout the state of Arizona.

Mr. Reppucci's areas of legal practice in family law includes, but is not limited to: marital dissolution (divorce); legal decision-making (child custody); parenting time (visitation); child support; spousal maintenance (alimony); community property; protective orders (restraining orders); annulments; legal separation; mediation; collaborative agreements; modification of existing family law agreements; and enforcement actions; and marital agreements such as a pre or postnuptial.

Mr. Reppucci understand the hardships associated with domestic legal concerns. He works diligently to not only help ensure that his clients achieve success in their family law concerns, but also goes to great effort to support them and help minimize the stress and emotional turmoil that accompanies divorce, child custody, and other legal family matters. While it is true there are times in life when we must all walk alone, this time is not when you are struggling with domestic legal problems.

WHAT ABOUT BOB?

The phone rang. The Caller ID on the phone screen identified the caller as Jerod, one of Bob's best friends. "Hello, this is Bob. What's up, Jerod?"

"Hey, is this a good time to talk?" his friend responded.

"Sure, any time is a good time to talk with one of my favorite people."

"Great. The reason I asked was I was worried about your wife being around and if you could talk, about... well...uh, anyhow—I was wondering who you were planning to use for your divorce lawyer because if you didn't know anybody I've got the name of a lady who did a great job for a colleague of mine."

"I'm not going to use one!" Bob responded arrogantly, overconfident as usual. "The way things look, this should be a piece of cake. I'm thinking we'll have it wrapped up in a month or two. Don't worry about me. I'll do fine. You know how lawyers are—nothing but troublemakers! I don't need some money-hungry lawyer charging me outrageous fees just so they can stir up the pot and make problems where problems didn't exist before they barged into the scene!"

Jerod paused, incredulous. "Did I just hear you say you are about to enter into one of the most potentially dangerous and critically important steps of your life and you don't think you should ask for professional assistance?"

Bob laughed. "You have me confused: The screen says, 'Jerod', but it feels like I'm talking to somebody named 'Negative Ned'. When did you become such a downer? You're usually a positive person."

Jerod, both flabbergasted and irritated at his friend's overconfident and dismissive approach to the situation, responded with "I'm not being negative, my friend; I'm being realistic and intelligent. Tell me, Mr. Fabulous, If you decided you are going to try and sail around the world and you have no experience with ocean sailing, would you hire a ship captain to help you who had a great deal of sailing experience?"

Bob, confused, responded with a tentative, "Of course I would. If I didn't, I wouldn't know what I was doing and I'd end up lost or shipwrecked or worse. The trip would certainly end up a disaster. Why ask such a weird question?"

Jerod returned with, "That's good to hear. I was worried you'd completely lost it. Second question: If you discovered you had cancer and needed surgery to cure it, would you operate on yourself or would you have a cancer doctor do it for you?"

"I'd have the doctor do it, of course! What's with these simpleton questions? What kind of idiot do you think I am?!" he exclaimed.

"At risk of offending, my friend," Bob said kindly, "you appear to be the kind of idiot who sees the wisdom of hiring a sea captain to help him navigate ocean waters and allowing a doctor to perform his medical procedures, but doesn't think he needs to hire a divorce attorney to help him navigate the potentially horrific waters of divorce. And the waters of divorce—

to stay with our nautical analogy—are waters that can crash The Good Ship Bob into a million pieces on the shore of life if not navigated properly. Please let me give you the name of this divorce attorney. I don't want to spend the rest of my life hearing you cry about how not using a lawyer destroyed your life!"

DIVORCE: THE BASICS

I write this book with two goals: The first is that some of you reading this decide you don't want to get divorced and begin a conversation between you and your spouse that results in both of you agreeing to "do the work" to make the changes in your lives that convert your failing marriage from into one that works.

The second is that those of you who decide to dissolve your divorce or pursue other family legal matters find this book helps make your divorce or other family law experience as positive as possible. Because of the incredible impact divorce will have on your life, I believe no one should try and go through this process by themselves. If you are contemplating divorce, the first step you should take is to meet with an experienced Arizona family law attorney. The divorce process can be stressful and lengthy. It overwhelms most people who try to do it without professional assistance. Please don't let yourself become the person who spends the rest of their life regretting their decision to not ask for help navigating the dangerous waters of divorce.

The laws of Arizona that govern divorce and other domestic (family) law matters can be quite confusing. It is always a good idea to discuss your situation with a legal professional who can ensure you know what to expect and what is required of you if you will be involved in family law proceedings. Whether you find yourself seeking or facing a divorce, legal separation, child support or legal decision-making (custody) order modification, or any other family law matter, it is essential you have a strong advocate by your side. Don't be like Bob and naively think you can handle this on your own. If you do, you will be heading blindly off into the wild blue yonder without a clue as to what you are doing. If you do choose to not be legally represented by a skilled family law attorney during your divorce or other family law issue, unnecessary stress and disaster are the likely outcomes. Divorces are usually quite messy and ex-spouses and ex-spouses in evolution generally have a very difficult time agreeing on important issues. Do yourself a favor and find a qualified family law attorney who will stand by you and help ensure you resolve what can be an extremely messy situation in a way that is fair for all parties involved, especially if children are involved.

CONCILIATION COUNSELING

Before diving headlong into the concept of ending your marriage and all that entails, please make sure you are both absolutely convinced you no longer desire to be married. In Arizona, either you or your spouse may file for what is known as *Conciliation Counseling* either before your divorce action begins or during the divorce proceedings. The purpose of conciliation counseling is to provide married couples free counseling to help them determine if they still possess a desire to save their marriage and if they are willing to work together to try and resolve their differences. Why go through the emotional, financial, and other struggles associated with divorce if spending some time together and working out your differences can save your marriage and prevent all that heartache?

There are three requirements for filing for conciliation counseling. First, you must be legally married in accordance with Arizona Law. Next, you or your spouse either have or have not filed a petition for divorce, legal separation or annulment. Finally, you must want to try and reconcile (get back together) or resolve the issues in your case with your spouse.

Just as with most aspects of divorce, the conciliation counseling process can be quite convoluted. Even not getting a divorce can be very complicated once the courts become involved because of its potentially confusing requirements. For example, one aspect of this court-related marital counseling process include a requirement that the two of you enter what is known as a "cooling off period". This is a period of sixty days where neither you nor your spouse may file any action for annulment, dissolution of marriage or legal separation. Also, if one of you files a petition for conciliation counseling after one of you has filed for divorce, your divorce proceedings are *stayed*, or "put on hold", while the courts work out details related to your case. And, although your marital dissolution action may be "stayed" (put on hold) until completion of your conciliation counseling, the counseling process has no affect on any spousal support or child custody orders previously issued by the court. As you can see, the ideal prevention for the disease known as divorce is prevention. If at all possible, attempt to sort out your marriage problems before they get to the place where you both believe your marriage must end.

That being said, let's begin by spending some time discussing the basics of divorce. Here are some terms and definitions you should know to better understand the divorce process.

REQUIREMENTS FOR DISSOLVING A MARRIAGE

"Dissolving a marriage" is the phrase for legally ending a marriage. When a divorce is complete, the marriage is considered legally dissolved and both parties are restored to the legal status of single persons. Arizona has four requirements for dissolving a marriage, granting an annulment, or granting legal separation:

First, one of the two parties in the divorce must currently live in Arizona and must have spent ninety days either living in Arizona or stationed in the Armed Forces in Arizona.

Second, the two of you must have demonstrated that you either failed in attempts to reconcile or amicably settle your differences or are not interested in reconciling or amicably settling your differences. The court will make sure both of you were advised that free counseling services (conciliation counseling) may be provided through conciliation services. If either of you believe this could be of benefit to your their marriage, then the marriage cannot be dissolved until such services were provided and failed. It is not necessary that both of you request a referral to conciliation services in order to receive this free counseling service.

Third, the two of you must state under oath that your marriage is *irretrievably broken* (there is no possibility of the two of you reconciling); or, if your marriage is a *Covenant Marriage*, you must demonstrate one of you violated the marriage by doing one of the following: (1) Committed adultery; (2) Committed a felony and have been sentenced to death; (3) Abandoned the marital home for at least one year; (4) Sexually or physically abused your spouse, child, or relative living with you or engaged in domestic violence or emotional abuse against one of these persons; (5) You and your spouse have lived apart for at least two years; (6) You and your spouse have lived apart for at least one year after filing for legal separation; (7) One of you habitually abuses alcohol or drugs; (8) Both of you agree you want to be divorced.

Fourth, the court has made final decisions regarding legal decision-making, *maintenance* of either spouse (alimony, child support) and how your money and property will be split up.

In addition, the court must know if the wife is pregnant at the time the marriage dissolution is granted, as this can obviously factor into numerous aspects of the divorce.

LEGAL SEPARATION

Legal Separation is where the court decrees that you and your spouse are not legally divorced, but both of you have the right to live apart with the rights and obligations of divorced persons. If you become legally separated, you and your spouse remain technically married and cannot marry other persons. You can *petition* (apply for) for a legal separation usually on the same basis as for a divorce, and may include requests for physical or legal custody, alimony, child support, and division of property. Couples choosing to pursue legal separation do so for many reasons, including strong religious objectives to divorce, worries about divorce-related stigma, or retained hopes of saving the marriage.

If you are legally separated and later choose to file for divorce, the terms of the separation agreement—except those providing for support, legal decision-making, and parenting time of children—will remain the same unless the court determines the current agreement is unfair. This is determined by considering you and your spouse's economic circumstances and any other relevant evidence either of you may produce.

If the court determines that your separation agreement is unfair as to disposition of property or maintenance, it may ask the two of you to submit a revised separation agreement or may make orders for the disposition of property of maintenance which has been deemed unfair.

Alternatively, if the Court finds that your separation agreement is fair regarding disposition of property or maintenance and is reasonable as to support, custody and parenting time of children, the separation agreement will be incorporated into the decree of marital dissolution.

UNCONTESTED VS CONTESTED DIVORCE

An *Uncontested Divorce* is where both you and your spouse agree to everything about the divorce and so there is no reason to involve the court system. Keep in mind that "everything" includes the things that usually cause problems for people wishing to no longer be married to each other, such as amount and duration of spousal maintenance (alimony), child support and parenting time if you have children, distribution of property, how you will resolve your marital debts, where each of you will live, and so on. Uncontested divorces are ideal because they are cost-efficient and generally much more amicable than contested divorces. Arizona courts require that you two agree: (1) your marriage is over because of an "irretrievable breakdown"; (2) on the division of your property and debts; and (3) whether one of you should pay alimony or spousal support and the amount. If children are involved, you will also have to decide on child support, parenting time, and both legal and physical custody. Resolving these issues between yourselves will save you a great deal on court costs and attorney fees.

A word of caution as regards uncontested divorces. While the idea of a peaceful, simple divorce sounds wonderful, don't allow yourself to settle for a poor outcome because you fear conflict or are intimidated by the idea of courtrooms, attorneys, or the stress of a prolonged divorce. Uncontested divorces are not a good idea if your marriage has been complicated by factors such as domestic violence, drug or alcohol abuse, irregular financial behavior, and other poor behavior by your spouse. Further, if the two of you cannot agree on things or you can't discuss the divorce amicably, your divorce is technically contested, thus eliminating the possibility of having an uncontested divorce.

A *contested divorce* is the opposite of an uncontested divorce. This is where one of you doesn't want to divorce or disagrees about some part of a proposed divorce settlement such as asset splits or spousal support. Once you have determined your divorce is "contested", you will have to involve the courts.

Another legal term it is important to know is *settlement*. Settlement occurs when you and your spouse begin a contested divorce, but the two of you end up agreeing ("settling") on the terms of the divorce. Again, these "terms" are how you will handle items such as child custody, alimony, property settlement, and other domestic matters described in the previous paragraphs. Achieving a settlement usually ends the litigation process started by the contested divorce because neither party will appeal the settlement. Happily, this means that your case doesn't have to be tried by a judge.

NO-FAULT DIVORCE

Arizona is a *no-fault divorce* state. This means you do not have to prove your partner is the reason you marriage is failing or failed (that they are the cause of an *irretrievable breakdown* in the marriage). The purpose having a no-fault system is it allows you and your spouse to focus on "positives" instead of "negatives". In essence, it changes the focus from punishing guilt to focusing on what the two of you believe has gone wrong in your marriage and how you can amicably resolve your issues and begin new lives as single persons. The "irretrievable breakdown" of the marriage standard is the only requirement for divorce in Arizona's no-fault based divorce. Obviously, a marriage that is irretrievably broken has no reasonable prospect of reconciliation.

The opposite of no-fault divorce is the *fault divorce*. Whereas the no-fault system avoids placement of blame, the fault system is predicted on placement of blame. Some examples of "faults" (reasons) for divorce in the fault system are domestic violence, sexual abuse, drug or alcohol abuse, or other behaviors that seriously damage or threaten your family's finances, safety, or ability to trust each other or feel comfortable living together.

COVENANT MARRIAGE

Covenant Marriage is a stricter form of marriage that is only available in a few states. Arizona is one of these states. Most marriages are *non-covenant marriages*, the term denoting marriages that are not "covenant". Covenant marriages are more difficult to enter or leave than non-covenant marriages. Because divorce is way of "leaving" a marriage, filing for divorce is more difficult if you have a covenant marriage. These difficulties include *covenants* (agreements between two parties) that must be met in order to get married or divorced that are not required in non-covenant marriages.

A covenant is an agreement between two parties. If you wish to enter into this type of marriage, you must agree to the “covenants”, or agreements, in covenant marriages that include: a written statement by each of you solemnly declaring that your marriage is a covenant between two people who agree to live together as husband and wife for as long as you live; you have chosen each other carefully and have received premarital counseling on the nature, purposes and responsibilities of marriage; you understand that a covenant marriage is for life; that if you experience marital difficulties, you will commit yourselves to making all reasonable efforts to preserve the marriage, including marital counseling; and, that with full knowledge of what your commitment means, you declare that your marriage will be bound by Arizona law on covenant marriages and you promise to love, honor and care for one another as husband and wife for the rest of your lives.

In addition to these declarations, you must also submit affidavits containing various other oaths and affirmations. Finally, there are specific signatory requirements you must meet in order for the covenant marriage to be recognized as valid.

PRENUPTIAL AGREEMENT

A *premarital agreement*, also known as a *prenuptial agreement*, is a legal contract made between two people before marriage designed to protect these individuals' property. Prenuptials detail items such as rights and privileges conferred by law on a surviving spouse; what each of you "brought" into the marriage—this would include property or other high-value items owned, income, inheritance funds, debts incurred prior to marriage, personal items owned prior to marriage, and other property. Prenuptial agreements are tools designed to protect assets. They are usually employed by couples where one spouse is significantly wealthier than the other, owns a business, or comes into the marriage knowing they are likely to become extremely wealthy. These agreements are usually permanent, but can contain time specifications. They must be in writing, reasonable, be very clear about the issues addressed in the agreement, and free from fraud.

The only reason for creating prenuptial agreements is the splitting of marital property associated with marital dissolution. Since Arizona is a community property state, all property earned or bought during marriage is split equally, with a few minor exceptions such as inheritance. Again, prenuptial agreements usually determine how to divide joint property; as such, they provide guidelines and isolate certain property outside of the marriage in certain cases.

Basically, a prenuptial agreement provides guidelines about how assets are to be split if a marriage fails. They contain items such as one spouse gets to keep certain assets if the marriage dissolves or a spouse is not required to assume any debts their spouse brought to the marriage. In the event of a divorce with a prenuptial agreement, this agreement helps determine how your marital assets will be divided. If one of you disagrees with the prenuptial at the time of divorce, your divorce is "contested" and must be settled in the courts.

MEDIATION

You and your spouse can avoid the court room process by hiring a lawyer known as a mediator. Mediation, also known as *Alternative Dispute Resolution*, is a "non-binding alternative form of dispute resolution where a [mediator] meets with parties and guides them to a mutually acceptable

resolution on the dispute." A mediator is a neutral party who will assist you and your spouse through the divorce process by giving you legal information and possibly some analysis, although they usually won't provide you with legal advice but may be willing to draft some of your required divorce papers.

Mediation is where two parties are brought together and guided by an independent person who helps them settle a dispute or controversy. Most disputed family law issues are subject to mediation. Mediation may be conducted by a private mediator agreed upon by you and your spouse, a mediator assigned by the court from a roster of mediators maintained by the court, or a mediator participating in an Alternative

Dispute Resolution (ADR) process overseen, administered, or approved by the court.

You and your spouse are free to select a private mediator by agreement. If you agree to private mediation, you sign and file a written notice with the court that private mediation will take place, the name of your mediator, and the date of your initial mediation conference. Alternatively, you may request that the court choose an independent mediator from a list of mediators supplied by them or from a roster of mediators maintained by the court. Unless otherwise ordered by the court or you and your spouse agree otherwise, the two of you will share the cost of mediation. Please be aware that this mediator may not conduct any subsequent family assessment or evaluation in the same case.

Mediation is not an option for everyone. The court may decline mediation if it believes mediation is not appropriate for your situation. Reasons for decline might include parental unfitness, substance abuse, mental incapacity, domestic violence, other good causes, or if the court believes mediation will cause undue delay in your case.

If the court refers or orders your case to mediation, you and your spouse must promptly notify the court when the mediation has concluded and provide all agreements you reached. In addition, although the court may require you to attend a mediation, actual good faith participation in the mediation itself is voluntary.

VIRTUAL MARRIAGE

We live in a world where people work, live, and meet online. The internet creates vast opportunities; it therefore makes sense that the concept of "internet marriage" eventually surfaced. Imagine this brave new world: a world where people who, for whatever reason, decide they wish to use the convenience of the internet to facilitate their marriage. A world where two people meet online, and whose entire relationship exists online decide they want to get married. Guess what? This is no science fiction story. Internet marriages are actually happening. The legal term for this kind of marriage is *virtual marriage.*

If a proposal is made virtually and it leads to a marriage where both of you are physically present, then this "virtual marriage" may be valid. However, at this time our legal system does not legally acknowledge a space-age love story where the two of you have never physically met. Virtual marriages that lack the formal requirements of a marriage license and a ceremony before an official are not considered valid marriages. A marriage that is purely virtual is not legally binding unless the marriage is officiated in reality. Translation: it doesn't matter how you met or dated, to be legally married both of you had to be physically present at a ceremony presided over by an official qualified to marry you.

This, then, begs the question of "Can you get divorced if you got married 'virtually'"? The simple answer is that you don't need to because people who weren't married to begin with do not need a divorce. Because virtual marriages are not considered legal marriages, they do not require a divorce.

ANNULMENT

There are two ways to legally end a marriage: (1) annulment; (2) divorce. An *annulment* is a *civil* (non-criminal) legal procedure which cancels a marriage between a man and a woman. A marriage that has been annulled is a marriage that has been completely erased. Legally, annulment declares that the marriage never happened: the marriage never technically existed and was never valid.

Civil annulments differ from divorces because annulment says there was something wrong with the marriage itself—that what everyone believed was a marriage was not a marriage. Arizona courts annul marriages for many reasons including: not obtaining a valid, official marriage license; one or both of you were intoxicated or somehow lacked the intent to enter into the marriage at the time of the marriage; one of you forced the other to get married; one of you was already married (bigamy); you are related by blood; you have failed to consummate the "marriage" (you have not had sexual relations); or one of you misrepresented his or her religion. The list of other possible reasons people seek marriage annulment is long and includes fraud, mental illness, underage marriage, and numerous others.

The reason annulment exists is because of the importance of legal *consent* in marriage. Legal consent is an action of reason and deliberation. A person who has the mental capacity to make an intelligent, well-reasoned decision demonstrates consent by performing an act required by somebody else.

Consent assumes the making of this decision will not be coerced by the other party and that the person "doing the consenting" is working with facts and has not been misled by the other party. Anything that may interfere with the consenting person being able to make an intelligent or correct decision may qualify as cause for annulment. If you look at the list of possible reasons (*impediments*) people are granted annulment, the underlying factor is always a problem with consent. The rationale for annulment always goes back to the argument that one of the parties did not "truly" consent to the union. And without true consent, people cannot be legally married.

This brings up the question of annulment versus divorce and which option you should pursue if you believe you have a case for annulment. The answer is ask the person you hired to help you make wise decisions throughout the process of ending your marriage: your attorney!

Annulment law in Arizona is tricky. In order to qualify for an annulment in Arizona you must be able to show that your marital agreement suffers from one of the *impediments* (see the non-exhaustive list in the previous paragraph) that render the marriage void. Again, keep in mind that annulment is different from divorce in that annulment says your marriage is "void", that it did not happen; whereas divorce says your marriage did happen, but that it didn't work out so you had it legally ended. It is also important you understand that by statute, the jurisdictional and procedural requirements for obtaining an annulment are the same as those for a divorce action. If your annulment action is successful and renders your marriage voidable, the court can divide your property so that each of you leave with the property you possessed prior to the voided marriage and may likewise determine matters related to any children you had during the marriage such as custody, parenting time, and child support.

This brings up what may be important consideration for you. If you are able to get your marriage annulled, the marriage will be considered unrecognized and so cannot result in division of community marital property. Why is this? Because if there was no marriage, there can be no marital property. So, if you wish to avoid application of the "equitable division (50/50)" marital property distribution that comes with every divorce action, you might want to consider annulment instead of divorce. Also, please understand that, while any given marriage may be "voided", your "marriage" does exist until one of you exercises his or her right to have it annulled.

ATTORNEY FEES

The court's job is to oversee divorce proceedings in an efficient and equitable manner. Anything or anybody who interferes with this process is at risk of being sanctioned by the court. Such sanctions can range from monetary penalties to jail time. The awarding of *Attorney Fees* may occur during your divorce proceeding if one of you offends the court. The purpose of awarding attorney fees in Arizona family court cases is based on the premise that a person who prolongs litigation by acting unreasonably should be sanctioned (punished) for such conduct.

The court takes many factors into account when granting or denying requests for reimbursement of attorney fees and court costs, including each spouse's financial situation and the reasonableness of their requests and conduct throughout the proceedings.

In addition, the Court may make you pay your

spouse's attorney fees and court costs if it determines that you:

1. Filed a petition in bad faith.
2. Filed a petition that was not grounded in fact or based on law.
3. Filed a petition for an improper purpose, such as to harass your spouse, cause an unnecessary delay in the divorce proceedings, or increase the cost of litigation to your spouse.

DIVORCE AND PERSONAL SAFETY

DOMESTIC VIOLENCE

Divorce is rarely a neat, clean-cut affair; it can cause a great deal of emotional turmoil. Splitting assets and fighting over custody of children or even pets are not uncommon. Domestic violence can be a reason for divorce and may also leave you with issues beyond the marriage.

Domestic violence is a term that can describe a wide array of abuse in marriage or a relationship. It can mean any act of violence or physical attack including sexual assault, hitting, and shoving; or emotional and financial abuse such as withholding money, isolating the partner from people, intimidation, uncontrolled anger, and taunting.

Arizona statutes define domestic violence broadly. Other acts included are harassment by phone or in person, stalking, intimidation, threatening words or conduct, kidnapping, criminal damage, disobeying a court order, photographing or recording a person in a private place or situation, disorderly conduct, and abusing a vulnerable adult or child.

As discussed before, Arizona is a no-fault divorce state. This is important as regards domestic violence because it means that neither spouse is required to provide a reason (domestic violence would be an example of a "reason") for a divorce. All you must do is demonstrate an irretrievable breakdown in your marriage. *Protective orders*, also known as restraining orders, are often employed when domestic abuse is a concern in a marriage or divorce proceedings. Protective orders are a ruling from the court designed to protect you from physical danger, harassment, or other danger at the hands of another person. A protective order is a civil court order that can be used to prevent the person abusing you from coming in contact with you in any way. This means that person cannot come near your home, work, school, or other locations included in the order.

There is a variety of protective orders you can seek if you have been the victim of domestic abuse in your marriage.

ORDERS OF PROTECTION

An Order of Protection is also known as a restraining order in Arizona. To receive an *order of protection*, a judicial officer must find that domestic violence has occurred and you have a specific relationship with the abuser. There are two main types of orders of protection:

1. Emergency Order of Protection (EOP): An EOP is intended to assist you if you are in immediate and present danger of domestic violence. A judicial officer has the power to grant an EOP in writing or orally.
2. Permanent Order of Protection: Before issuing a permanent order of protection, a formal hearing will be held before a judicial officer. Both you and your spouse are allowed to present your cases. The permanent order will last for one year from the date it is served upon your abuser. After that year expires, you can seek to renew the order if the threat of domestic violence remains.

The order of protection can be structured so as to prevent the abuser from having any sort of contact with you—whether by phone, in person, or otherwise. If you live together, the abuser will have to move out. The abuser may also be required to turn in his or her firearms and may be prevented from contacting the children. If the abuser violates any terms of the protective order, he or she can be placed in jail.

You should consider seeking a protective order from the court if you believe you or your children are being abused or are in danger from your spouse. Protective orders can help keep you safe because they can result in the court ordering safety measures such as law enforcement officers being assigned to accompany you when you go to your home to get belongings; preventing your abuser from committing domestic violence; preventing your abuser from having contact with you in any way—this includes texts and telephone calls; and forcing your abuser to turn in any firearms or other dangerous weapons in his or her possession.

The same "Safety first!" rules regarding domestic violence and abuse apply regarding treatment of your children. For most parents, the only thing they fear more than being hurt by their spouse is harm coming to their children. Just as with yourself, do not hesitate to seek a protective order if you believe your spouse is a threat to your children. Do everything you legally can to keep your child or children away from a violent environment. You can obtain a temporary emergency custody order if you need to get away from an abusive spouse immediately. Courts will seriously consider the best interests of your child/children when making custody and parental decisions. As with all divorce matters, it is generally best if your attorney handles this aspect of your divorce.

ADDRESS PROTECTION

If you are like other people experiencing domestic violence and other forms of marital abuse, you may already be hiding from or wish to hide from your abusive spouse. The courts can help with this issue by not telling your spouse where you are living or staying. The legal name for this type of legal protection is *address protection*. The purpose of address protection is to provide protection to litigants and children subjected to domestic violence.

If you desire address protection, your attorney will file a request with the court stating that you reasonably believe that physical or emotional harm may befall either you or your minor child or children if your spouse finds out where you are living or staying. If this protection is granted, the court shall make sure your address is not publicly disclosed until the court orders otherwise.

UNIQUE SITUATIONS IN DIVORCE

GREEN CARDS

Divorce and immigration law often intersect. *Green cards* are greatly prized by non-US citizens (also known as *foreign nationals*) because they allow foreign nationals to work and live permanently in the US, even though having the green card does not make them a US citizen. It is understandable that the possible effects of divorce on green card status can become a major concern that can turn divorce proceedings—a process that is often very messy—into an extremely complicated situation.

Persons seeking to marry solely for the purpose of obtaining a green card quickly discover that the system seriously discourages such behavior. Foreign nationals not possessing a green card who attempt to marry a US citizen are required to satisfy a significant number of requirements designed to thwart attempts to use marriage as an avenue for obtaining a green card.

The divorce process in a marriage involving a green card can greatly complicate the life of the foreign national involved, with much of this depending on the timing of the divorce. Suffice to say, the green card issue will be a major issue for you if either you or your spouse obtained their green card through your marriage and you seek a divorce. This is yet another case where having the professional guidance of a divorce attorney is highly recommended for all persons going through the divorce process.

BIGAMY

Bigamy is when you marry someone else while you are already married. Arizona law defines bigamy as "a person having a spouse living who knowingly marries any other person." This is a serious charge and is a class 5 felony. Even though the only requirement for divorce in a no-fault divorce state such as Arizona is an an irretrievable breakdown in your marriage, Arizona courts are so offended by the idea of bigamy that you may want to consider using bigamy as grounds for divorce if you are the victim of bigamy. That being said, your divorce attorney may encourage you to pursue annulling your marriage instead of divorce because the courts may determine that, because of the bigamy your marriage was never valid to begin with.

If you are the person accused of bigamy, you have a couple of potential defenses in Arizona. First, bigamy charges may not apply if your previous spouse has been absent for five years and you didn't know they were still alive or if it was your understanding that the previous marriage had been legally ended by annulment, divorce, or other court judgment. Because Arizona law says finding you guilty of bigamy requires that you knowingly performed the illegal act, if you honestly and reasonably believe your prior marriage was terminated you could also argue that you made a mistake. Other potential arguments include not having a valid previous marriage to begin with because you can only be prosecuted for bigamy if there was an actual previous marriage. Accordingly, cohabitation and other non-marital relationships cannot result in a charge of bigamy. There are also other possible defenses, but understand that a bigamy charge is serious and could result in incarceration if you are found guilty. If you have been charged with bigamy, immediately contact an experienced family law attorney.

SAME-SEX MARRIAGE

Social change is a constant in America. One recent change is *same-sex marriage*. Arizona is a state that recognizes marriage between same-sex couples.

Regardless of the sex of a marriage's members, getting married creates the unfortunate prospect of divorce. Just as with traditional marriage, the only requirement for same-sex divorce in Arizona is showing an irretrievable breakdown in the marriage. However, because some states accept the notion of same-sex marriage and some do not, it stands to reason that a state which refuses to recognize same-sex marriage would not be willing to entertain the notion of divorce in this type of relationship. This state-to-state disconnect regarding same-sex marriage can result in a wide array of potential legal complexities. For example, if a same-sex couple gets married in Arizona and then moves to state which does not recognize same-sex marriage, the couple may not be able to obtain a divorce in that state. Arizona and most other states have a residency requirement that says that one of the parties must currently live in Arizona to file for divorce.

As if the miseries of relationship problems aren't

enough, same-sex marriage couples who find themselves thwarted in their efforts to divorce due to state-to-state legal issues may also become mired in other potential ramifications, including issues with end-of-life decisions, child care, distribution of property at death, and the desire to remarry. Obviously, same-sex marriage can be very complicated and, just as with traditional marriage, makes having the guidance of an experienced family law attorney all the more critical.

DIVORCE AND COMMUNITY PROPERTY

INTRODUCTION TO COMMUNITY PROPERTY

Divorce involves more than ending a relationship. You must also confront the complexity of dividing property and assets. Because Arizona is classified as a community property state, property is generally divided equally during a divorce. Examples of exceptions to this rule would include a spouse who wasted a large part of the marital assets through gambling, drug or alcohol abuse, or other irresponsible behaviors.

When you choose to file for a dissolution of your marriage, your property must be divided. In the United States, property division is managed in one of two ways: Some states are separate property states; some are community property states. Arizona is a community property state. *Community property* is marital property that belongs to each spouse equally and retains that characterization upon

divorce. Specifically, community property is any property acquired during the marriage, with limited exception. In community property states like Arizona, upon divorce community property is split equally among the spouses.

Moving from state to state can complicate property division manners in divorce if the states in question manage property division differently. Examples of these type of "complications" might include: any property you have in a separate property state will continue to be separate property unless the state follows a quasi-community property rule. A *quasi-community property rule* is a rule that applies in Arizona. In this instance, the separate property that would have been community property will now be characterized as community property. In Arizona, property acquired in a separate property state can be considered community property.

INTELLECTUAL PROPERTY

Division of marital property is one of the most potentially divisive issues in divorce proceedings. Stories abound of couples incurring legal costs many times the value of the "stuff" they are fighting over in an effort to make sure their spouse does not end up with these spoils of the marital war. Because Arizona is a *community property state*, this means that marital assets—the definition of *marital assets* being assets accumulated acquired after the marriage—are divided equitably between spouses.

Splitting your assets can be easy or incredibly difficult depending on your personal situation. Property such as your home, vehicle, or any other property earned during the marriage will be classified as marital property and will be subject to splitting. Unfortunately, disposition of *intangible property*, with "intangible" meaning you can't see it or touch it, can be much more complicated.

Intellectual property is intangible property that can come in many forms and involve many areas of law such as property and privacy law and touch on both state and federal law. Arizona is a community property state, which means that all marital property except for things such as inheritance will be split equally between the couple. Thus, if you were to conceive a brilliant idea or create an invention during the marriage, the idea or invention will most likely be considered community property and be split between you and your spouse. For example, if you expend most of your energy creating a copyrighted work before the marriage then it should be your separate property. However, if you expended the energy and created the copyright during the marriage then it is community property.

Intellectual property is typically split into four categories: patents, copyrights, trademarks, and trade secrets. Although many don't realize it, almost everyone has some form of intellectual property that affects their life. Here is a brief overview of the various types of intellectual property.

1. Patents are temporary (20 year) monopolies granted to inventors who make new, novel, non-obvious, useful processes, machines, articles of manufacture, compositions of matter, and sometimes business methods. In exchange for the temporary monopoly the inventor must disclose "what the invention is" and "how to make it" to the general public. Patents are difficult to obtain because of high cost, long wait times, and the first-to-file system.
2. Copyright Law protects original works of authorship that are fixed in a tangible medium of expression. Your artistic work is copyrighted the moment you create it, and this form of intellectual property can cover music, sound recordings, computer software, video games, books, fashion design, and more. Your copyright will last for your lifetime plus 90 years after your death. Copyrights may also be registered for more protection.

3. Trademarks are words, phrases, symbols, designs, or a combination of these that identify the source of goods from one party to another. There are also service marks that identify a service instead of a product and trade dress which covers the distinctiveness of your product's appearance. Examples of trademarks include names such Coca Cola®, Xerox®, and Google®. Generic names cannot be protected but the more unique the name the stronger the protection. You can also federally register your trademark to gain more protection over it.
4. Trade secrets are governed by federal law and cover a wide variety of information that has value because it is kept secret. This includes formulas, patterns, programs, devices, compilations, techniques, and processes as long as you make a reasonable effort to maintain such secrecy. Some of the most well-known trade secrets are the Coca Cola recipe and Google's search algorithm.

Dividing intellectual property can be very complicated. The ability to split this type of property between divorcing spouses oftentimes depends on the type of intellectual property involved and multiple other factors which include, but are not limited to: whether you and your spouse were named as co-authors or joint owners for copyright; whether you and your spouse owned a business and were both named on the patent(s) or equally owned trademark rights; whether your intellectual property was licensed; what the value of your intellectual property is; and so on. For example, patent earnings are typically brought through royalties which may be divisible in a divorce. Thus, you and your spouse will need to be flexible when working out not only the value of intellectual property, but how it is to be split between the two of you. As you can easily see, intellectual property division has the potential to be very divisive—especially if the "property" in question is of great value. Property division is yet another aspect of divorce that illustrates why choosing to be represented by competent legal counsel is wise, because not doing so can be very costly!

RETIREMENT

Another critically important property settlement issue in divorce is retirement benefits. Retirement benefits differ from disability payments in that disability payments are considered separate property of the disabled spouse. The characterization of your marriage, divorce, and type of retirement benefits are all factors that help determine how your retirement benefits will be divided upon the dissolution of your marriage.

Because Arizona is a community property state, most properties gained by you and your spouse during your marriage will be split equitably between the two of you. The same rule applies to retirement benefits. How your property will be classified is based on when and how it was acquired, with limited exceptions. If you were married for the entire time that your employer provided you retirement benefits, your retirement benefits are community property. Conversely, if you earned your retirement benefits outside of the marriage they are considered separate property.

There are different financial vehicles (plans) that can make up a retirement plan. Pension plans are tax-deferred savings plans that contribute to your retirement and are considered community property in a divorce. A defined benefit plan (DBP) is a type of pension fund that is controlled by your employer which pays you monthly income at retirement for the rest of your life. The contributions to this plan made by you and your employer while you are employed are tax free and accumulate over time.

Other common types of retirement plans include military retirements and railroad retirements. While military retirements are almost always considered community property, railroad retirements are not subject to community property division.

A *Qualified Domestic Relations Order*, known as a QDRO, is a legal order entered as part of a divorce or legal separation that splits and changes ownership of a retirement plan to give the divorced spouse their share of the asset or pension plan. Most retirement plans require the ex-spouse to file a QDRO with an administrator before any portion of the participant's retirement plan can be paid to the ex-spouse. The court can award any portion of the retirement plan by issuing a QDRO which the plan must obey. A QDRO can be used for many things, such as assigning retirement benefits under more than one retirement plan for the same or a different employer.

WILLS

Wills are another important part of a community property settlement. Be aware that not only can divorce cut you off from many things you hold dear such as friends, family, and children, it can also wreak havoc in your life via its effects on your will and estate. Worst case scenarios can result in one spouse being "cut out" entirely.

Estate planning tools such as a *last will and testament*, commonly known as a will, provide instruction as to how a person who died wished their assets distributed upon their death. If the will is found to be invalid and there is not another valid will, the deceased person's estate will pass *intestate*. Intestate laws in Arizona say that if you have a spouse but no descendants or you do have descendants from that spouse, then your spouse will inherit everything. However, if you had children or descendants that were not from your spouse, your spouse will inherit half of your separate property but will not receive the community property that belonged to you, while your children will inherit the other half of the separate property and half of the community property that belonged to you.

DIVORCE AND MARITAL DEBTS

Responsibility for marital debts is a significant concern for most couples going through a divorce proceeding. The court assigns responsibility for certain *community property obligations* (debts) in your property settlement agreement or decree of dissolution of marriage or legal separation. These allocations are done equitably by the Court, meaning both parties generally receive one-half of the debt obligation.

Unfortunately, while most people think having a marital debt agreement issued by the court settles the issue of how your marital debts will be managed, the harsh financial reality is that if either parent fails to pay off any of their debt obligations, both parties are "on the hook" for that obligation. Unfortunately, a court-ordered marital debt agreement generally does not remove either spouse from personal obligation for these debts because they are considered a separate contract between the spouses and their creditors—"creditors" being institutions such as banks, credit unions, credit card issuers, utility companies, finance companies, medical providers, retailers, and others. Because these creditors are not parties involved in your court case, they are not bound by court orders or agreements for repayment of such obligations, so they can hold both of you responsible for the marital debt.

Here's an example illustrating a possible outcome of a disputed marital debt: A divorcing couple has a credit card debt of $5,000. The marital debt agreement handed down by the court orders that the husband should pay this debt and he must agree to indemnify and hold the wife harmless as regards this debt. Several months after the divorce the wife receives a letter from the credit card company demanding she pay off the entire credit card debt immediately. They inform her that no payments have been made on the debt and the debt obligation has now increased to $5,500 because of monthly interest charges. The furious wife calls the husband to ask him what's going on and he casually informs her that he has not made any payments on this debt and has no plans to ever make any payments towards the satisfaction of this debt.

The wife is bewildered because she thought the marital agreement removed any possibility of her having to pay anything on this debt. The wife can take her ex-husband back to court over his contemptuous behavior to seek enforcement of the court's agreement that he settle this debt; however, for the reasons stated earlier she could find herself deciding to make monthly payments on this obligation in order to keep this debt from negatively affecting her credit.

Another marital debt issue regularly encountered in divorce proceedings is education-related debts. In general, because Arizona is a community property state, student loan debt incurred during the marriage is *community debt* (shared by both spouses), so the spouse that was not the student will be required to pay half of the other spouse's student loan debt. That being said, the court will often consider many factors when determining education-related debt such as timing of the divorce, whether a contract or agreement existed between the spouses, increase in one spouse's future income because of the education, and whether the marriage benefited from the education

DIVORCE AND SPOUSAL SUPPORT

SPOUSAL MAINTENANCE (ALIMONY) BASICS

Divorce is a life changing-event for everyone in your family. Depending upon your individual circumstances, you might lose the financial support of the primary breadwinner following a divorce, be forced to move from the family home, have to share time with your children, and divide possessions. Recognizing the serious financial and other shifts that so often accompany a divorce, the Arizona legislature has adopted the concept of *alimony*, which is also known as *spousal maintenance*. Alimony is defined as ongoing payments from one spouse to the other. The intent of spousal maintenance is to help ensure the divorce is as equitable and fair as possible and enable the spouse with fewer financial resources to successfully transition to the next phase of his/her life.

Alimony is a way to "level the playing field" following a divorce. In many marriages one spouse will sacrifice personal, professional or educational opportunities for the benefit of the household. For instance, you and your spouse may have agreed that one of you will stay home with the children while the other pursues a higher-paying job. If you end up divorcing, the stay-at-home spouse will be at a financial disadvantage because he or she will have fewer professional opportunities due to their sacrifices made during the marriage. In this and other similar cases, a court could issue an award of alimony to the former stay-at-home spouse until that spouse can adequately support him or herself.

If you are the stay-at-home spouse in this instance, it is quite clear that without alimony you will experience great difficulty moving forward after the divorce. This example illustrates one of the reasons for selecting an experienced family law attorney: their job is to use their experience and knowledge to aggressively represent you in your pursuit of a spousal maintenance award so you can start your new life in the best possible economic position.

There are two types of alimony in Arizona: *Temporary alimony*, also known as *alimony pendente lite*, is a court-ordered temporary spousal maintenance while an action for separation or divorce is pending. Temporary alimony is the most commonly awarded type of alimony and is granted at the court's discretion during the divorce proceedings. It is intended to provide for the immediate needs of the spouse with fewer financial resources during the divorce. Temporary alimony usually ends when the divorce becomes final, although it can be extended.

Permanent alimony may be granted for as long as the court deems necessary. This type of alimony is awarded much less frequently than temporary alimony, is usually reserved for spouses with long-term needs, and generally only awarded when the marriage was lengthy.

Alimony in Arizona is complex and the court is allowed great discretion in determining the amount and length of any alimony award. The court can order either a one-time lump sum payment or periodic payments.

As with most other aspects of divorce, couples have the option to negotiate their own alimony as part of their divorce settlement. In a divorce settlement, you are in control of dictating and agreeing on a reasonable alimony award. Divorce settlements may include agreement as to an alimony sum—sometimes in exchange for a property division arrangement that benefits the compromising party.

If you are going through a divorce or planning to go through a divorce, you are probably aware of spousal maintenance. Because the issue of spousal maintenance and child support often go hand in hand, it is important you have a good understanding of spousal maintenance before learning about child support. If your marriage is one where the two of you made the decision that one of you would stay home and care for the children while the other one worked to support the family, spousal maintenance will likely become a consideration. As previously discussed, *spousal maintenance*—also called spousal support or alimony—may require the higher earning spouse in your marriage to pay money to the spouse who depended financially on the income of the other spouse because of the marriage. In other words, if the dependent spouse cannot pay living expenses, the judge may require the spouse earning a higher income to pay money to the dependent spouse for a certain period of time. Again, the court decides whether these payments occur in a one-time lump sum or are distributed periodically. In addition, if the court determines that you must pay alimony to your spouse and you believe the amount should be changed either because you believe the original award was unfair or because your financial situation has changed, you may ask the court to change the amount by filing a petition with the court.

The court considers numerous factors when determining spousal maintenance. In deciding whether maintenance is needed in your marriage, a court may consider how much has been contributed to the other spouse's educational opportunities, whether the dependent spouse has enough assets or property to provide for his or her needs, and whether or not the spouse in question is self-sufficient. This determination is also likely to include evaluating the current economic environment and individual factors such as age, years married, and the lifestyle you two have become accustomed to living now as compared to before you were married. The court incorporates many factors into its spousal maintenance decision-making process; the actual amount awarded is very fact-sensitive and will depend on your individual case.

There are two broad categories of spousal maintenance in Arizona: (1) temporary; and (2) permanent. In some cases, the judge may order a temporary form of spousal maintenance *during* the divorce proceeding. Judges usually consider spousal maintenance to be a temporary rehabilitative measure designed to help the dependent spouse in your family financially survive the divorce process and get back on their feet after the divorce. Most dependent spouses achieve this goal by obtaining skills and education that help them obtain employment sufficient to support themselves and their family.

Most couples dissolving their marriages are unlikely to encounter a situation resulting in permanent spousal maintenance. This type of alimony—one that results in spousal maintenance of long or permanent duration—is rarely awarded in today's court system. When it is awarded, it's usually in situations involving divorcing couples of advanced age, where the dependent partner suffers from significant health issues, or when this same partner evidences a complete lack of earning potential.

If your situation involves enough liquid assets, you may find a property settlement more desirable than either temporary or permanent spousal maintenance. When choosing a property settlement in lieu of alimony, the settlement will assign a value to a spouse's depleted income and give a monetary award based on those values. Property settlements often depend on whether or not the divorce is contested or uncontested.

DIVORCE AND CHILD SUPPORT

DETERMINING CHILD SUPPORT

When children are factored into divorce there are many more things to consider than how you split your property and other marital possessions. Child support exists to provide your child or children with financial support because it is morally and ethically right to do so. Parents who contribute financially to their children's life are much more likely be active in other areas of their life, as well. All that aside, it is public policy in Arizona that a parent must be responsible for their dependent children.

Child Support Guidelines help establish child support standards. Child support applies to all children, including those born out of wedlock or adopted. The court understands that each family's situation is unique, so determining the duration and amount of child support depends on your situation and other factors such as the age of your children, your income levels, and numerous other factors.

When you are a parent you have a legal duty to support minor children (under age 18) by providing for them financially. If you are the parent receiving child support, it is critical you understand that managing the funds designated for child support is a serious responsibility. These funds are to be used to provide your children a place to live, education, clothing, medical care, and more. The amount of child support you will either receive or pay will be determined in part by the unique factors related to you and your ex-spouse's personal situations.

The Child Support Enforcement Program (CSE) is a program that helps make sure parents pay their child support obligation by assisting in the enforcement of collection of agreed-upon child support payments. If you are a parent who has been ordered by the court to pay child support to your ex-spouse, it is very important you understand that if you are found guilty of knowingly not providing adequate support for your child without a valid excuse you will be found at fault of a class 6 felony—a charge that may result in your incarceration. Do not take this responsibility lightly. Not only is it your duty as a parent to take care of your children in every way possible, including financially; making an active decision to not fulfill this obligation will seriously complicate your life.

If you are having difficulty paying your child support due to work loss, illness, or other factors resulting in financial hardship, you should immediately make the court aware of your situation to prevent your possible arrest and other possible legal complications. While the court will not tolerate laziness, drug or substance abuse, or other self-serving behaviors resulting in failure to fulfill child support obligations, it is reasonable and will consider multiple factors when determining whether you had an acceptable excuse such as your assets, earnings, and effort you made to obtain funds to pay your court-ordered child support obligation.

The Arizona Child Support Guidelines are based on the financial resources and needs of the child and of each parent, the standard of living the child would have enjoyed in a two-parent household, and the allocation of parenting time.

The child support amount is primarily based on the adjusted gross incomes of both you and your spouse, as well as the amount of parenting time each of you receives with your children. The income of a parent's new spouse is not counted or included as income of the child's parent.

While adjusted gross income and parenting time are the main two determinants in any child support calculation, be aware that the court may factor in other items such as court-ordered spousal maintenance paid or received; court-ordered child support paid or received from other sources; medical, dental, or vision insurance premiums; child care costs; non-common children supported by the parties without court order; extraordinary expenses for the common minor children; and more.

Arizona courts use an *Income Shares Model* to determine child support. This model calculates child support amount by first determining each parent's gross income, adjusting it, then combining the two to determine your family's *Combined Adjusted Gross Income*. The number of children you have together is also incorporated into this calculation. The court also includes other expenses when determining the total child support amount, such as education, medical insurance, and childcare expense. This final figure, the

Total Child Support Obligation, is divided among both parents according to each parent's adjusted gross income and then adjusted again for costs associated with parenting time.

Determining each spouse's gross income is determined by including all their sources of income. The court's guidelines state that these sources include, but are not limited to "income from salaries, wages, commissions, bonuses, dividends, severance pay, pensions, interest, trust income, annuities, capital gains, social security benefits... worker's compensation benefits, unemployment insurance benefits, disability insurance benefits, recurring gifts, prizes, and spousal maintenance." If your income fluctuates, it will be *annualized* (estimated for the year). If one of you is self-employed, owns a partnership, or is part of a closely-held corporation then that spouse's gross income is gross receipts minus ordinary and necessary expenses required to produce the income.

As you can readily see, child support determination can become very complicated. It is yet another aspect of the marital dissolution process where having a trained legal expert representing your interests is critically important, because these determinations will affect you and your children's quality of life for many years.

An important term in child support determination is *Self-Support Reserve*. This "reserve" is the minimum amount allowed for child support. This amount may deviate at times. The Court uses the *Self-Support Reserve Test* to verify that the noncustodial parent is financially able both to pay the child support order and maintain at least a minimum standard of living.

To calculate your self-support reserve, simply deduct the sum allotted for the deduction from the noncustodial parent's (parent the children do not live with) adjusted gross income. If the resulting amount is less than the child support order, the court may reduce the current child support order to the amount calculated by the reserve test after first considering the financial impact this reduction would have on the custodial parent's household. Another method for calculating your self-support reserve amount is with the state's online child support calculator.

http://www.azcourts.gov/familylaw/2015ChildSupportCalculator.aspx

LEGAL DECISION-MAKING (CHILD CUSTODY)

INTRODUCTION TO LEGAL DECISION-MAKING

One of the many potentially divisive factors in a divorce is legal decision-making (child custody). The court considers a multitude of factors when determining what is in the best interest of your child or children when it comes to legal decision-making. Unfortunately, legal decision-making issues persist for many couples after the marriage is dissolved, so it is best for everyone involved—especially the children—if you two reach a mutually acceptable agreement.

Arizona made some major changes to its legal decision-making laws in 2013. These include:

1. Replacing the word "custody" in favor of the term "legal decision-making";
2. There are now two types of legal decision-making: (1) sole and (2) joint;
3. "Legal decision-making" is now defined as "both parents share decision-making and neither parent's rights or responsibilities are superior except with respect to specified decisions as set forth by the court or the parents in the final judgment or order." This should help reduce confusion and agitation between divorced spouses because earlier definitions of "custody" covered both the legal (decision-making) and physical (parenting time) components of child "custody", which often led to confusion when the two parties did not understand the two separate aspects of the issue. The new law should alleviate this past problem now that "legal custody" is defined as "Legal Decision-Making" and "parenting time" is simply called "Parenting Time".

4. Parenting Time is now defined as "the schedule of time during which each parent has access to a child at specified times. Each parent during their scheduled parenting time is responsible for providing the child with food, clothing and shelter and may make routine decisions concerning the child's care." Therefore, time exercised between child and parent is now considered "Parenting Time" and not "Visitation".
5. "Visitation" is now defined as "a schedule of time that occurs with a child by someone other than a legal parent."

There are numerous child custody-related legal terms you need to know. The legal term for "child custody" in Arizona was recently changed to *legal decision-making*. You will likely see these terms used interchangeably during your marital dissolution process. Do not let this confuse you: both mean the same thing.

Physical custody is having actual physical possession of the child. Physical custody dictates where your child will reside and how much time they will spend with each parent. In Arizona, parents who do not have primary physical custody of the child will be given visitation rights or continuing contact with the child unless the situation requires limitations. This aspect of physical custody is called *parenting time* because it describes when the non-custodial parent gets to spend time with your child.

Legal custody determines who has the responsibility to make legal decisions for your child. Examples of such decisions would include: religious, non-emergency medical, education, extracurricular affairs, and some personal care decisions. If *joint legal decision-making* is awarded, this responsibility is shared, meaning both parents must work together to make these decisions about their child's welfare. Also, in joint legal decision-making agreements both parents must agree to a court-approved *parenting plan* that outlines each parent's rights and responsibilities for the personal care of the child, how decisions are to be made, and a plan for resolving disputes that may arise.

The alternative to joint legal decision-making is *sole legal decision-making*. This type of custody is less commonly seen than joint legal decision-making and means that one parent has no legal decision-making role in the child's life. However, sole legal decision-making agreements usually provide parenting time for the non-custodial parent. In today's legal environment, the most common reason sole legal decision-making is granted to one parent is because the court believes one of the parents should not be responsible for making decisions about critically important issues in the child's life.

One other legal decision-making possibility that is rarely employed is *in loco parentis*. This term means that someone or some group "stands in for the parent". This unique legal decision-making arrangement is usually employed when both parents are mired in severe life challenges and the court believes neither of them should be responsible for guiding their children's care or important life decisions.

DETERMINING LEGAL DECISION-MAKING

Again, joint legal decision-making means both parents share decision-making and neither parent's rights or responsibilities as regards making decisions related to their child's welfare are superior to that of the other parent. By contrast, sole legal decision-making means one parent has the legal right and responsibility to make major decisions for a child and the other parent does not.

The court considers many factors when determining which legal decision-making arrangement is appropriate, including:

1. The past, present, and potential future relationship between the parent and the child.
2. The interaction and interrelationship of the child with the child's parent or parents, the child's siblings, and any other person who may significantly affect the child's best interest.
3. The child's adjustment to home, school and community.
4. If the child is of suitable age and maturity, and what the child would prefer as regards legal decision-making and parenting time.
5. The mental and physical health of all individuals involved.

6. Which parent is more likely to allow the child frequent, meaningful, and continuing contact with the other parent.
7. Whether one parent intentionally misled the Court during the divorce proceedings in order to cause unnecessary delays, increase cost of litigation, or attempt to persuade the Court to give a legal decision-making or a parenting time preference to that parent.
8. Whether one of the parents has perpetrated domestic violence or child abuse on a family member.
9. The nature and extent of coercion or duress used by a parent in obtaining an agreement regarding legal decision-making or parenting time.
10. Whether either parent was convicted of certain crimes.

SUBSTANCE ABUSE AND LEGAL DECISION-MAKING

Substance abuse is considered a serious concern as regards legal decision-making. If the court determines that one of you has persistently abused drugs or alcohol or has been convicted of certain drug offenses within twelve months of the request for legal decision making or parenting time, it will likely decide that joint or sole legal decision-making by that parent is not in the best interests of a child. The simple translation of this is if you are a parent who wants to remain involved in the life of your child, do not abuse alcohol or drugs or engage in criminal behavior. The opposite side of this coin is if you are a parent who believes your spouse should not be allowed much time with your children and your spouse has drug or alcohol problems or a criminal history, this presents an opportunity for you. This is yet another example of where having an experienced family law attorney by your side can make a major difference in you and your child's life.

The Court considers many factors related to substance abuse when determining legal decision-making. These include, but are not necessarily limited to: (1) the facts presented at the time of trial supporting that a parent abused drugs or alcohol or was convicted of such offenses; and (2) the facts presented at the time of trial that the legal decision-making or parenting time arrangement ordered by the Court appropriately protects a child from harm associated with their spending time with or being under the care of a parent known to have been convicted of substance abuse or related criminal convictions.

Please understand that if you are a person with a history of substance abuse issues or have substance-abuse related criminal convictions, you have the burden of demonstrating to the court why these substance abuse-related reasons for reducing or denying your legal decision-making privileges do not apply in your case and why your children's safety would not be compromised while in your care and/or by the decisions you may make on their behalf.

LEGAL DECISION-MAKING AND MILITARY DEPLOYMENT

Because the United States is generally involved in numerous military conflicts around the world, military deployment is an important issue in family law—especially as relates to legal decision-making. Many couples involved in divorce proceedings are interested in knowing whether a military deployment can be considered a good reason for making changes to already-established legal decision-making terms.

Arizona law states that the "Court shall not consider a parent's absence caused by deployment or mobilization or the potential for future deployment or mobilization as the sole factor supporting a real, substantial and unanticipated change in circumstances". While this phrase sounds like it removes military-related parental absence from being considered as a reason for altering legal decision-making arrangements, in reality this provision does not restrict the ability of the Court from modifying parenting rights and responsibilities on a temporary basis during an absent parent's deployment or mobilization. Examples of how the court might address these kinds of situations might include the Court modifying such rights if:

1. A military parent who has legal decision-making or parenting time has received notice from military leadership that the military parent will deploy or mobilize in the near future.
2. The deployment or mobilization would have a material effect on the military parent's ability to exercise parental rights and responsibilities or parent-child contact.

LEGAL DECISION-MAKING: RELOCATION TO ARIZONA

Another issue that may arise during the process of determining how legal decision-making responsibilities for your children will be decided by the court is recent relocation of your children from another state to Arizona. For legal decision-making to be determined in Arizona, your children must meet certain conditions as described below. If your children do not meet these requirements, then you must either wait until you can satisfy one of the conditions or you will have to commence your legal decision-making action in the state that has jurisdiction over your matter. This is usually the state where the child lived before moving to Arizona.

Arizona courts require any one of the following to be true in order to make legal decision-making determinations:

Arizona is the home state of the child on the date you began the legal decision-making proceeding or was the home state of the child within six months before the commencement of the proceeding and the child is absent from this state but a parent or person acting as a parent continues to live in this state.

A court of another state does not have jurisdiction or a court of the home state of the child has declined to exercise jurisdiction on the ground that this state (Arizona) is the more appropriate state for the legal decision-making decision and both of the following are true: (a) The child and the child's parents, or the child and at least one parent or a person acting as a parent, have a significant connection with this state other than mere physical presence; (b) Substantial evidence is available in Arizona concerning the child's care, protection, training and personal relationships.

All courts having jurisdiction under paragraph 1 or 2 have declined to exercise jurisdiction on the ground that an Arizona court is the more appropriate forum to determine the legal decision-making of the child.

A court of any other state would not have jurisdiction under the criteria specified in paragraph 1, 2 or 3.

As you can see from reading these complicated rules, it's not always exactly clear whether Arizona is the right place to initiate a legal decision-making action. Once again, you see why it makes sense to have an experienced family law attorney on your side prior to initiating your desired legal decision-making action.

LEGAL DECISION-MAKING: RELOCATING MINOR CHILDREN

While some of the statutes governing child support and parenting time are complicated and confusing, the rules related to relocating minor children are relatively clear. If the court believes the proposed relocation is in the child's best interests, it is likely to be approved. If the court believes the motive behind the proposed move is to spite the other parent, it will likely deny the relocation and may sanction the parent attempting to "harm" the other parent through the proposed relocation. If both parents are entitled to joint legal decision-making or unsupervised parenting time and both parents reside in Arizona, at least sixty days' advance written notice shall be provided to the other parent before a parent may relocate the child outside the state or relocate the child more than one hundred miles within the state. Parents who violate this statute without good cause can be sanctioned by the court. This sanction may include a reduction in the offending parent's legal decision-making responsibilities or parenting time.

If you are a parent who has been informed by your spouse that they wish to relocate your child, you may petition the court to block this move. The court considers the following when determining whether to allow a parent to relocate a minor child:

1. The 10 factors outlined on pages 42 and 43 in the Determining Legal Decision-Making section of this book.
2. Whether the relocation is being made or opposed in good faith and not to interfere with or to frustrate the relationship between the child and the other parent or the other parent's right of access to the child.
3. The prospective advantage of the move for improving the general quality of life for the custodial parent or the child.
4. The likelihood that the parent with whom the child will reside after the relocation will comply with parenting time orders.
5. Whether the relocation will allow a realistic opportunity for parenting time with each parent.
6. The extent to which moving or not moving is likely to affect the emotional, physical or developmental needs of the child.

7. The motives of the parents and the validity of the reasons given for moving or opposing the move, including the extent to which either parent may intend to gain a financial advantage regarding continuing child support obligations.
8. The potential effect of relocation on the child's stability.

LEGAL DECISION-MAKING: THIRD-PARTY REQUESTS FOR AUTHORITY

On rare occasions, a *Third-Party* (non-parent) in Arizona may ask the Court if it can be awarded legal decision-making authority for a child and/or place a minor child in their care. These cases generally result when a family is severely fractured and both parents are experiencing severe personal or other challenges. Examples of parental challenges that could result in a third-party requesting to take over legal decision-making might include the parents struggling with severe drug or alcohol abuse, domestic violence, criminal behavior, severe physical or mental illness, and so on. While courts generally agree it is usually in the best interests of a child for their parents to provide rearing, there are situations where the facts clearly demonstrate it would likely be significantly detrimental to the child if they were to remain or be placed in the care of either legal parent.

Satisfying the requirements for awarding a third-party legal decision-making authority or placement of a child in their care is very difficult. This is understandable, because when the court awards these rights and responsibilities to a non-parent, they are taking the children away from both parents. First, the third-party must demonstrate an *in loco parentis* (acting in place of the parent) relationship between themselves and the child. In addition, they must also demonstrate several other factors in their petition to have a chance of being awarded legal decision-making. Meeting these requirements is difficult and legal decision-making is usually only awarded to third-parties in very severe circumstances.

LEGAL DECISION-MAKING: BEST INTEREST ATTORNEYS

A *best interest* attorney is a lawyer appointed by the court for the purposes of protecting the best interests of the child. There are many reasons the court may consider taking such an action, but all result from the court believing that neither of their parents is able to perform this role. Arizona courts may appoint a best interest attorney for the benefit of a minor child subject to a domestic relations actions for a number of reasons. These include allegations of abuse or neglect; the parents being persistently in significant conflict with one another; a history of substance abuse by either parent; history of family violence; serious concerns about the mental health or behavior of either parent; the child is an infant or toddler; the child has special needs; or any other reason deemed appropriate by the court.

If a best interest attorney is appointed in your case, you may be at serious risk of having your parental rights seriously reduced or even terminated. This person will be permitted to participate in the conduct of the litigation to the same extent as everyone else involved in the case. A best interest attorney may also submit a report to the court and/or testify concerning their findings at the time of any hearing scheduled by the court.

It is important you understand that a best interest attorney does not work for you or your spouse/ex-spouse. In many cases, quite the opposite is true. In essence, this person works for your child because their job is to protect that child. Understandably, a best interest attorney can have a substantial impact on the outcome of any case. For this reason it is strongly suggested that if you are a parent involved in a domestic relations case where a best interest attorney is appointed by the court that you seek immediate consultation with an experienced attorney in order to better to protect your interests.

LEGAL DECISION-MAKING: MODIFYING CHILD SUPPORT

Requests to modify (change) existing child support arrangements are a common reason people seek out a family law attorney. These people are frequently shocked to discover that the reason or reasons they believe their legal decision-making arrangement should be changed will not be accepted by the court. The Arizona rules governing modifications of legal decision-making state you must wait at least one year from the date of your last legal decision-making decree before you can request it be changed. Exceptions to this rule include:

1. If you believe your child's present environment may seriously endanger their physical, mental, moral or emotional health.
2. Domestic violence involving spousal abuse or child abuse has occurred since your last joint legal decision-making order.
3. A parent has been charged with a dangerous crime against children, child molestation, or an act of domestic violence in which the victim was a minor.

While the court is eager to do everything it can to protect the rights and welfare of children, it punishes parents whose sole motivation when filing for change of legal decision-making is inflicting emotional, financial, or other harm upon their ex-spouse. Be aware that if you file a petition for modification of legal decision-making and your motive for doing so is not to improve the welfare of your child, the court may assess attorney fees and costs against you if it finds that the modification action is vexatious and constitutes harassment.

LEGAL DECISION-MAKING: MEDICAL MARIJUANA

The medical marijuana issue is not just a hot-button political, medical, and moral issue—it is also a subject increasingly encountered in family courts during legal decision-making. Even though this issue is relatively new in Arizona family courts, the following statute is used by the court when evaluating legal decision-making and parenting time rights when one or both of the parents utilize marijuana as medical treatment: "No person (that is a qualified medical marijuana patient) may be denied custody of or visitation or parenting time with a minor, and there is no presumption of neglect or child endangerment for conduct allowed under this chapter, unless the person's behavior creates an unreasonable danger to the safety of the minor as established by clear and convincing evidence."

While this statute is helpful because it clearly states that a person cannot be arbitrarily denied custody and/or parenting time just because they are a medical marijuana patient, the fact that it does not clearly define the "behavior or behaviors" that present an unreasonable danger to the safety of a minor child is not helpful. Unfortunately, the statute dumps this difficult decision into the lap of the courts. And, because courts are conservative and tend to err on the side of caution when issues are unclear—especially in the case of child welfare issues, this vague definition tends to work against qualifying medical marijuana patients attempting to maintain and protect their parenting and legal decision-making rights.

PARENTING TIME

PARENTING TIME: VISITATION RIGHTS

By itself, being involved in a divorce can cause you to feel like your life is on fire. Add child-related issues to this fire and this fire can explode into an inferno. Fortunately, regardless of legal decision-making arrangement, Arizona parents are granted *Parenting Time* (visitation rights). The purpose of parenting time is to ensure the child has healthy contact with both parents. The court typically approaches determining parenting time by balancing many factors, such as the child's age, a parent's willingness to visit the child, and in some cases whether the parent who does not have legal decision-making (non-custodial parent) needs the supervision of another person during visitation.

Visitation rights in joint legal decision-making situations are usually decided between the parents outside of the court. One of the keys to facilitating parenting time agreements outside of the court is that both of you make reasonable requests for parenting time. These requests should keep in mind that both parents should be included as much as possible in important events such as school breaks, holidays, birthdays, and other special events. Parents who feel they are being "cut out" of their children's lives are likely to become parents who can make resolving parenting time issue a nightmare in terms of court time, unhappy children, stress, and attorney costs. Also, if the two of you are unable to come to a parenting time agreement then the court will take over and make the decision for you. As with most issues related to children and parents, family courts are hesitant to completely deny a parent contact with their child. They will consider doing so, however, when extreme circumstances demand it. Examples of extreme situations include abuse of the custodial parent, abuse of the child, or if visitation poses danger to the child.

Noncompliance with parenting agreements is unacceptable to the court. When this occurs, the non-violating parent must alert the court in order for the court to become involved in the issue. In Arizona, if a parent violates visitation rights by not showing up at their designated visitation, he or she will be given a reasonable opportunity to explain the violation. If the court determines that the parent did not have good cause for violating the visitation rights, the court may order parental education or family counseling at the violating parent's expense or even request that both parents attend mediation. The court can also make any other decision it wishes as long as it is in the best interest of the child—decisions that may include a fine or holding the other parent in contempt of court.

PARENTING TIME: PARENTING PLANS

Parenting plans are used in disputed family court cases to settle legal decision-making and parenting time issues. When the court adopts a parenting plan, it spells out the exact legal decision-making terms the parents must follow and provides them with parenting time terms that attempt to simultaneously maximize parenting time for both parents and protect the best interests of their minor child. Moreover, even if both parents agree to a parenting plan, the court can mandate inclusion of other elements and/or factors into a parenting plan it deems necessary to promote and protect the emotional and physical health of a child.

Every parenting arrangement either agreed to by the parties or ordered by the court in Arizona must comply with specific parameters. These parameters outline the minimum requirements of what your parenting plan must contain. One good rule of thumb regarding these plans is that the more aspects of your minor children's lives your plan addresses, the more likely the plan will be successful. This is a worthy goal, because well-constructed parenting plans that "work" for both parents are key to minimizing future contacts with the court.

Although not meant to be an exhaustive list of all requirements, at a minimum, a parenting plan should include the following:

1. A designation of the legal decision-making as joint or sole as more fully set forth and defined by statute.
2. Each parent's rights and responsibilities for the personal care of the child and for decisions in areas such as education, health care and religious training.
3. A practical schedule of parenting time for the child, including holidays and school vacations.

4. A procedure for the exchanges of the child, including location and responsibility for transportation.
5. A procedure by which proposed changes, disputes and alleged breaches may be mediated or resolved, which may include the use of conciliation services of a superior court or private mediation or alternate dispute resolution services.
6. A procedure for periodic review of the plan's terms by the parents.
7. A procedure for communicating with each other about the child, including methods and frequency.
8. A statement that each party has read, understands and will abide by the notification requirements set forth by particular statutes.

Also, one thing some divorcing couples find confusing is that shared legal decision-making does not necessarily mean equal parenting time. Again, *legal decision-making* is the term related to issues such as with whom and where the child will live, and the school they will attend; whereas *parenting time* addresses the amount of time the parents will spend with the child, where that time will be spent, and so on.

PARENTING COORDINATORS

A *Parenting Coordinator* is a professional appointed by the court to help parents resolve disputes regarding parenting issues and make recommendations to the court when parents can't come to an agreement on these conflicts. Many parents find parenting coordinators extremely helpful because having a knowledgeable, unbiased professional make reasonable recommendations to the court about your children is much preferable to suffering the emotional strain and financial cost associated with repeated trips to court to resolve disputed issues.

You should consider hiring a parenting coordinator when your attempts to resolve parenting issues through the courts and other avenues have failed. Experienced parenting coordinators are skilled at resolving disagreements over scheduling, overnight parenting time, choice of schools, extracurricular activities, exchanging of children, holiday or vacation scheduling, and other issues important in family life.

Parents assigned a parenting coordinator who worry about the power this person can have on their personal and family life are relieved to learn that the court places limits on their power. These limits include their being precluded from recommending substantive changes to the parenting plan, with one example being that they cannot propose changes to legal decision-making authority.

PARENTING TIME: NEED FOR INTERVIEWING CHILDREN

Many parents involved in legal decision-making and parenting time disputes want to know if their children will be required to appear or speak in the court during any court proceedings. You will be happy to know that your child will not be forced to speak in open court. However, if the court decides it wants to know your child's opinion on court matters, it can choose from options that allow their opinion to be heard without exposing them to the stress of testifying in open court or having to face a parent or other person they are afraid of or that makes them uncomfortable. One such option is privately interviewing the child in the judge's chambers to determine the child's preferences on legal decision-making and parenting time. Another option is having a court-appointed professional evaluate the minor child. These interviews may be conducted at any point during the proceedings and are usually recorded by either a court reporter or other electronic medium.

The court has the power to prevent these interviews from being heard by any party, including the parents and their attorneys. However, the court will only do this when it believes allowing the child's testimony to be heard by the forbidden party could result in harm to the child. An example of this would be when the court proves through the child's protected testimony that one of the parents has been "coaching" the child's answers or punishing the child for voicing their wishes.

SUPERVISED PARENTING TIME

The court has the power to mandate *Supervised Parenting* Time. This is done when the court believes that leaving the child alone with one of the parents could harm the child's health or emotional development. Supervised parenting time mandates that a social service agency or mental health professional be involved with a family to make sure parenting time and legal decision-making orders are followed. These duties may include supervising or overseeing the parenting

time periods. In some cases, the exchange of the child is supervised by a third party to diminish the conflict between the parents to which the child would be exposed without supervised exchanges.

POSSIBLE EFFECTS OF DOMESTIC VIOLENCE ON PARENTING TIME

Aside from the potential ramifications of a criminal conviction, a parent who is violent towards their child or ex-spouse is at risk of having their parenting time reduced or terminated. The court considers the safety and well-being of a child to be of primary importance. For obvious reasons, the court considers evidence of certain acts of domestic violence contrary to the best interests of the child, and will likely reduce or even terminate the offending parent's parenting time if charges of domestic violence are substantiated.

Arizona courts consider the following factors when evaluating a domestic violence accusation for purpose of determining either legal decision-making and/or parenting time:

1. Findings from another court of competent jurisdiction.
2. Police reports.
3. Medical reports.
4. Child protective services records.
5. Domestic violence shelter records.
6. School records.
7. Witness testimony.

SELECTING YOUR FAMILY LAW ATTORNEY

This book makes it clear that trying to handle your divorce or other family law matters on your own is unwise. And choosing the right attorney is even more important than making the decision to have an attorney represent your interests. Because the results of your divorce will affect every remaining day of you and your children's lives, it is critical that your family law attorney be experienced, knowledgeable, and someone you can comfortably communicate with.

So how does someone like you who may have never used the services of an attorney go about picking this person who is going to protect you in this critically important event in your lives? Selecting your lawyer is more than just picking a name; it means establishing a close and sensitive relationship that will continue for months and perhaps years.

First, start by asking other professionals for their recommendations. Lawyers, accountants, psychotherapists, religious leaders and other professionals meet and work with divorce lawyers in the course of their work and are usually a reliable referral source. Lawyers are the ideal place to start because they are aware of other lawyers' reputations. If you need a divorce lawyer outside your geographical area, divorce lawyers in your area often know the best people in other locations.

Next, ask official organizations such as your state bar and the American Bar Association. Look for attorneys with specialty credentials because they have usually passed an examination in this area of the law. The American Academy of Matrimonial Lawyers is an organization with a rigorous screening procedure that admits only qualified specialists.

Seek referrals from other persons. Friends who have gone through a divorce are often a good resource; however, keep in mind that every client and every case is different, so it is difficult to know how a lawyer will perform for you based on someone else's case because your case will be different than theirs. Also, because the lawyer-client relationship is highly personal, you should meet the lawyer and make your own determination as to whether you feel the lawyer's personality and practice style is a good fit for you.

Other factors to consider when making your divorce attorney decision include:

Cost. The rules relating to divorce attorney cost are:

1. There is a wide variety in what divorce attorneys charge for their services.
2. The better-known and more well-established the attorney, the more they usually charge.
3. There are often highly-skilled and experienced lawyers available who charge less because they are not yet well known. A lawyer in this category can be an excellent value.

Your goal in this first meeting is to interview the attorney and decide if they are the person you should hire. It's unlikely you will be able to make a good decision if the lawyer's focus is not listening to the details of your case, but selling you on their services.

Professional credentials are very important. Don't pay excessive attention to long lists of professional organizations on a lawyer's website because inclusion in most professional organizations requires only that the person be a lawyer and pay their annual dues. A much better indicator of professional prominence and quality is active participation in the lawyer's area of practice. Publishing articles, books and treatises on family law and teaching other lawyers are excellent indicators of experience, competence and reputation. Also, look for lawyers who have been practicing family law for many years because experience is the best teacher.

Do not choose your attorney without interviewing them personally. During the interview, make sure the attorney provides you time to thoroughly discuss your situation. Take the following with you to this meeting: a list of your assets, debts and sources of income; a copy of your last several years' tax returns; a written narrative detailing the important events in your relationship with your spouse; and a list of the questions and things you want to cover during the interview. Make sure you write down the answers to these questions. Finally, do not feel rushed to make an immediate decision. Take your time with this, because this decision will have significant ramifications on your life.

In the same vein, if you are not comfortable with a lawyer you interview for any reason, you should probably trust your instincts and not hire that person. Be sure the lawyer is someone you can talk to and who listens to you. Keep in mind you will be telling the lawyer intimate facts of your life and they may offer you advice and information you may not like that will help your case.

Also, while it may sound trite, the location of your lawyer's office may be very important because it is nice to be able to go conveniently to your lawyer's office to meet and work on your case. Also, if the lawyer's office is a great distance from the courthouse, you may have to pay for their travel time.

Again, thank you for taking the time to read this book. I hope it has been helpful in the management of your family law concern.

Sincerely,

Ryan M. Reppucci

NOTES:

Printed in Dunstable, United Kingdom

91222521R00067